BARCELONA

SHOPS & MORE

BARCELONA

SHOPS & MORE

Angelika Taschen

Photos Pep Escoda

TASCHEN

HONG KONG KÖLN LONDON LOS ANGELES MADRID PARIS TOKYO

EL Raval

8   Mercat de la Boqueria
14   La Portorriqueña
20   Ras
24   Barcelona Reykjavík
30   Manantial de Salud
34   Curtidos Pinós
40   Sastrería El Transwaal

Barri Gòtic
El Born
La Ribera

54   Xocoa
60   Caelum
66   Antiga Cereria Lluís Codina
72   La Manual Alpargatera
78   Gotham
82   Papabubble
88   Cafés El Magnífico
92   La Pelu
96   Brunells
102   Demasié
106   E & A Gispert
112   Targa
116   Lobby

L'Eixample
Gràcia
Sant Gervasi

128   Llibreria Altaïr
132   Loewe
136   Floristería Navarro
140   Charcuterías Joaquín Gracia
146   Josep Font
150   Vinçon
156   Kowasa
160   Coriumcasa
166   Camper
170   Jean Pierre Symbol
174   Jean Pierre Bua
180   Cristina Castañer
184   Oriol Balaguer

192   Imprint / Impressum

El Raval

8 Market hall/Markthalle/Halle de marché
Mercat de la Boqueria

14 Coffee roasters/Kaffeerösterei/Torréfacteur
La Portorriqueña

20 Architectural & art books/Architektur- & Kunstbücher/
Livres d'architecture et d'art
Ras

24 Bakery/Bäckerei/Boulangerie
Barcelona Reykjavík

30 Herbalist/Kräuterladen/Herboristerie
Manantial de Salud

34 Haberdashery & interior/Kurzwaren & Interieur/Mercerie & intérieur
Curtidos Pinós

40 Cooks' apparel/Gastronomiebekleidung/Vêtements de cuisine
Sastrería El Transwaal

Mercat de la Boqueria

Plaça de la Boqueria
La Rambla 85–89, 08001 Barcelona
☎ +34 93 318 25 84
www.boqueria.info
Metro: L3 Liceu; L1, L3 Catalunya

La Portorriqueña

Carrer d'en Xuclà 25, 08001 Barcelona
☎ +34 93 317 34 38
Metro: L1, L3 Catalunya

Ras

Carrer del Doctor Dou 10, 08001 Barcelona
☎ +34 93 412 71 99
www.rasbcn.com
Metro: L3 Liceu; L1, L2 Catalunya

Barcelona
Reykjavík

Carrer del Doctor Dou 12, 08001 Barcelona
☎ +34 93 302 09 21
www.barcelonareykjavik.com
Metro: L3 Liceu; L1, L2 Catalunya

GALETA
CIVADA
PLATAN
COCO

Manantial
de Salud

Carrer d'en Xuclà 23, 08001 Barcelona
☎ +34 93 301 14 44
www.manantial-salud.com
Metro: L1, L3 Catalunya

Curtidos Pinós

Carrer de l'Hospital 79, 08001 Barcelona
☎ +34 93 317 63 84
www.curtidospinos.com
Metro: L3 Liceu

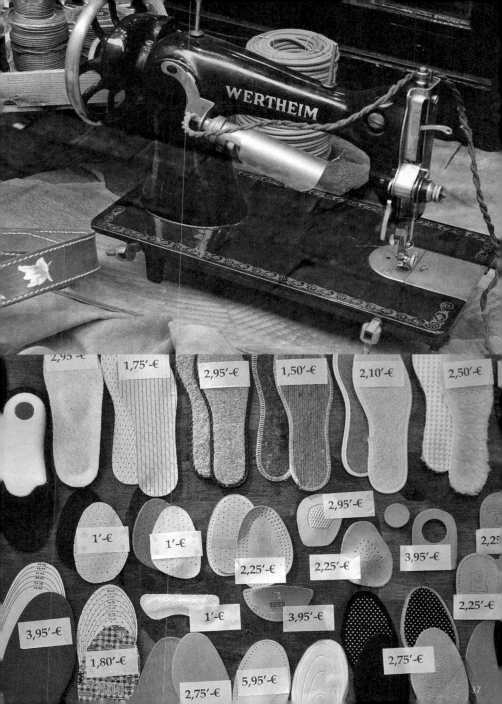

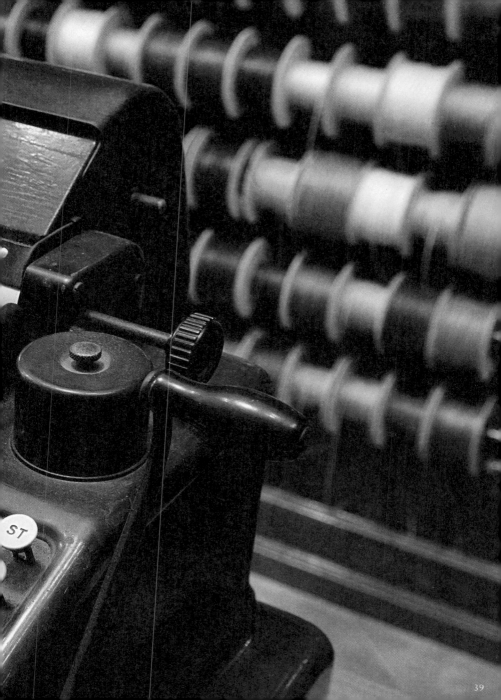

Sastrería
El Transwaal

Carrer de l'Hospital 67, 08001 Barcelona
☎ +34 93 318 65 94
Metro: L3 Liceu

Mercat de la Boqueria

Plaça de la Boqueria
La Rambla 85–89
08001 Barcelona
☎ +34 93 318 25 84
www.boqueria.info

pp. 8/9

Traditional Spanish Market
Interior: 332 stalls

Open: Mo–Sa 8am–8.30pm | **X-Factor:** The market bar "Pinotxo".
Hawkers were selling their wares here as early as the 13th century – today La Boqueria is still quite an institution and offers the freshest products in the city.

Öffnungszeiten: Mo–Sa 8–20.30 Uhr | **X-Faktor:** Die Marktbar „Pinotxo".
Schon im 13. Jahrhundert verkauften fliegende Händler an diesem Ort ihre Waren – heute ist La Boqueria immer noch die Institution und bietet die frischesten Lebensmittel der Stadt.

Horaires d'ouverture : Lun–Sam 8h–20h30 | **Le « petit plus » :** Le café du marché « Pinotxo ».
Au XIIIe siècle, les marchands ambulants proposaient déjà leurs marchandises en ce lieu. Demeurée une véritable institution, La Boqueria offre les produits les plus frais de la ville.

La Portorriqueña

Carrer d'en Xuclà 25
08001 Barcelona
☎ +34 93 317 34 38

pp. 14/15

Freshly Roasted Coffee since 1902
Interior: 1960s

Open: Mo–Sa 9am–2pm and 5–8pm | **X-Factor:** The "mezcla de la casa".
This shop owes its name to the founder's Puerto-Rican wife. She roasted the coffee beans shortly before they were sold – a rule that holds to this very day.

Öffnungszeiten: Mo–So 9–14 und 17–20 Uhr | **X-Faktor:** Die „mezcla de la casa".
Seinen Namen verdankt dieser Laden der puerto-ricanischen Frau des Gründers. Sie röstete die Bohnen erst kurz vor dem Verkauf – diese Regel gilt noch heute.

Horaires d'ouverture : Lun–Dim 9h–14h et 17h–20h | **Le « petit plus » :** La « mezcla de la casa » | Ce magasin doit son nom à la femme du fondateur, qui était portoricaine. Elle avait coutume de ne moudre les grains de café qu'au moment de la vente. Cette règle est toujours en vigueur.

Ras

Carrer del Doctor Dou 10
08001 Barcelona
☎ +34 93 412 71 99
www.rasbcn.com

pp. 20/21

Books on Art & Architecture
Interior: Futuristic polycarbonate shelves

Open: Tu–Fr 11am–9pm | **X-Factor:** The gallery.
The shop belongs to the Barcelona publisher Actar – in addition to Actar titles, it also sells other books on art and architecture as well as avant-garde magazines.

Öffnungszeiten: Di–Fr 11–21 Uhr | **X-Faktor:** Die Galerie.
Der Shop gehört dem Barceloneser Verlag Actar – neben eigenen Titeln werden auch weitere Bücher über Kunst und Architektur sowie Avantgarde-Magazine verkauft.

Horaires d'ouverture : Mar–Ven 11h–21h | **Le « petit plus » :** La galerie.
La boutique appartient à la maison d'édition Actar qui, outre ses propres titres, propose ici des ouvrages sur l'art et l'architecture ainsi que des magazines d'avant-garde.

Barcelona Reykjavík

Carrer del Doctor Dou 12
08001 Barcelona
☎ +34 93 302 09 21
www.barcelonareykjavik.com

pp. 24/25

Delicious Homemade Bread & Pastries
Interior: Simple cottage charm

Open: Mo–Fr 10am–9pm; Sa 10am–4pm | **X-Factor:** Only organic ingredients are used here.
The oven-fresh bread and pastries are available in savoury (for example, with dried tomatoes) or sweet variations.

Öffnungszeiten: Mo–Fr 10–21, Sa 10–16 Uhr | **X-Faktor:** Hier werden nur biologische Zutaten verwendet.
Die ofenfrischen Brote und Leckereien gibt es in salzigen Varianten (etwa mit getrockneten Tomaten) oder süß aromatisiert.

Horaires d'ouverture : Lun–Ven 10h–21h, Sam 10h–16h | **Le « petit plus » :** Tous les ingrédients sont bios.
Les pains et autres gourmandises sorties tout droit du four existent en version salée (aux tomates séchées par exemple) ou sucrée.

Manantial de Salud

Carrer d'en Xuclà 23
08001 Barcelona
☏ +34 93 301 14 44
www.manantial-salud.com

pp. 30/31

Curtidos Pinós

Carrer de l'Hospital 79
08001 Barcelona
☏ +34 93 317 63 84
www.curtidospinos.com

pp. 34/35

Healing Herbs & Natural Cosmetics
Interior: Nostalgic

Open: Mo–Fr 9am–2pm and 4–8pm; Sa 9am–2pm |
X-Factor: The list of herbs is available in English, French and German.
This Catalan family business has been treating all sorts of ailments with naturopathy for over 80 years.

Öffnungszeiten: Mo–Fr 9–14 und 16–20, Sa 9–14 Uhr |
X-Faktor: Die Kräuterliste ist auf Englisch, Französisch und Deutsch erhältlich.
Mit katalanischen Naturheilmitteln kuriert der Familienbetrieb seit mehr als 80 Jahren alle Leiden.

Horaires d'ouverture : Lun–Ven 9h–14h et 16h–20h,
Sam 9h–14h | **Le « petit plus » :** La liste des plantes est disponible en anglais, français, allemand.
Depuis plus de quatre-vingts ans, l'entreprise familiale guérit tous les bobos avec ses plantes catalanes.

Dry Goods in a Shop from the 19th Century
Interior: Includes antiques, such as Wertheim sewing machines

Open: Mo–Fr 9am–2pm and 4–8pm; Sa 9am–2pm |
X-Factor: The woven leather bands.
Originally a shoemaker's, this shop now offers an apparently inexhaustible range of haberdashery.

Öffnungszeiten: Mo–Fr 9–14 und 16–20, Sa 9–14 Uhr |
X-Faktor: Die geflochtenen Lederbänder.
Ursprünglich eine Schuhmacherei, bietet dieser Laden ein scheinbar unerschöpfliches Sortiment an Kurzwaren.

Horaires d'ouverture : Lun–Ven 9h–14h et 16h–20h,
Sam 9h–14h | **Le « petit plus » :** Les tresses en cuir.
Cordonnerie à l'origine, ce magasin propose un immense choix en articles de mercerie.

Sastrería El Transwaal

Carrer de l'Hospital 67
08001 Barcelona
☏ +34 93 318 65 94

pp. 40/41

Custom-made Uniforms for Chefs & Waiters
Interior: Pure 1920s

Open: Mo–Fr 9.30am–1.30pm and 4.30–8pm;
Sa 9.30am–1.30pm | **X-Factor:** The classic aprons – also for amateur cooks.
Equipping Cooks & Co since 1888 with made-to-measure uniforms. Owner Rosa Ferrer gives outstanding advice.

Öffnungszeiten: Mo–Fr 9.30–13.30 und 16.30–20,
Sa 9.30–13.30 Uhr | **X-Faktor:** Die klassischen Schürzen – auch für Hobbyköche.
Seit 1888 stattet man hier Köche & Co. mit Maßuniformen aus. Die Inhaberin Rosa Ferrer berät hervorragend.

Horaires d'ouverture : Lun–Ven 9h30–13h30 et
16h30– 20h, Sam 9h30–13h30 | **Le « petit plus » :** Les tabliers classiques, également pour les cuisiniers amateurs.
Depuis 1888, confection sur mesure des uniformes de cuisine.
La propriétaire Rosa Ferrer est de très bon conseil.

Barri Gòtic
El Born
La Ribera

54 Chocolate shop/Schokoladengeschäft/Boutique de chocolats
Xocoa
(Map on page 6)

60 Boutique & tea salon/Boutique & Teesalon/Boutique & salon de thé
Caelum

66 Candles & devotional articles/Kerzen & Devotionalien/
Cierges & objets de dévotion
Antiga Cereria Lluís Codina

72 Espadrilles/Espadrilles/Espadrilles
La Manual Alpargatera

78 Vintage furniture/Vintage-Möbel/Mobilier vintage
Gotham

82 Handmade sweets/Hausgemachte Bonbons/Bonbons maison
Papabubble

88 Coffee roasters/Kaffeerösterei/Torréfacteur
Cafés El Magnífico

92 Trendy coiffeur/Trendiger Friseur/Coiffeur à la mode
La Pelu

96 Pastry shop/Konditorei/Pâtisserie
Brunells

102 Cookies/Kekse/Biscuits
Demasié

106 Imported speciality foods/Kaufmannsladen/Épicerie
E & A Gispert

112 Kitchenware/Küchenwaren/Ustensiles de cuisine
Targa

116 Concept store/Concept Store/Concept Store
Lobby

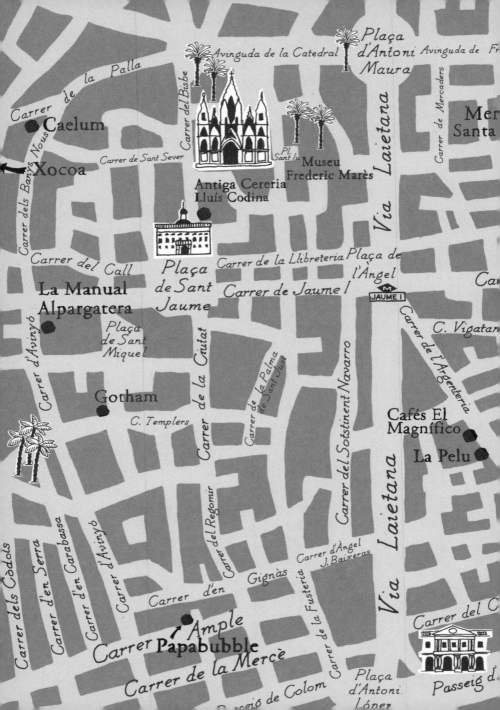

Carrer de la Palla

Avinguda de la Catedral

Plaça d'Antoni Maura

Avinguda de Fr

Carrer del Bisbe

Carrer de Mercaders

Carrer

Caelum

Mer
Santa

Carrer dels Banys Nous

Xocoa

Carrer de Sant Sever

Pl.
Sant Iu

Museu
Frederic Marès

Via Laietana

Carrer de Mercaders

Antiga Cereria
Lluís Codina

Carrer del Call

Carrer de la Llibreteria

Plaça de
l'Àngel

Car

La Manual
Alpargatera

Plaça
de Sant
Jaume

Carrer de Jaume I

JAUME I Ⓜ

Carrer d'Avinyó

Plaça
de Sant
Miquel

Carrer de la Ciutat

Carrer de l'Argenteria

C. Vigatan

Gotham

C. Templers

Carrer de la Palma
de Sant Just

Carrer del Sotstinent Navarro

Cafés El
Magnífico

La Pelu

Carrer d'Avinyó

Via Laietana

Carrer del Regomir

Carrer de la Fusteria

Carrer d'Àngel
J. Baixeras

Carrer dels Còdols

Carrer d'en Serra

Carrer d'en Carabassa

Carrer d'Avinyó

Gignàs

Carrer del C

Carrer d'en

Ample

↗ Papabubble

Carrer
Carrer de la Mercè

Passeig d

Plaça
d'Antoni
López

Passeig de Colom

el Pellisser

Carrer d'en Giralt

mbó

e
na

Carrer d'en

Carrer dels Carders

Carrer d'en Tantarantana

Plaça de
l'Acadèmia

Carrer del Comerç

Passeig de Pujades

Carrer dels Assaonadors

la Princesa

Demasié

unells

Carrer del Rec

Carrer de Montcada

Carrer dels Flassaders

Carrer de la Fusina

Picasso

la Ciutadella

Carrer del Comerç

Carrer Comercial

de

Parc de

dels Sombrerers

Passeig del Born

E & A
Gispert

Carrer del Comerç

Lobby

Passeig

de

Carrer del Rec

Carrer de
l'Esparteria

Carrer de la Ribera

Targa

del Mar

Pla de

Palau

Avinguda del Marquès de l'Argentera

Estació de França

Xocoa

Carrer de Petritxol 11–13, 08002 Barcelona
☎ +34 93 301 11 97
Metro: L3 Liceu

Caelum

Carrer de la Palla 8, 08002 Barcelona
☎ +34 93 302 69 93
Metro: L3 Liceu

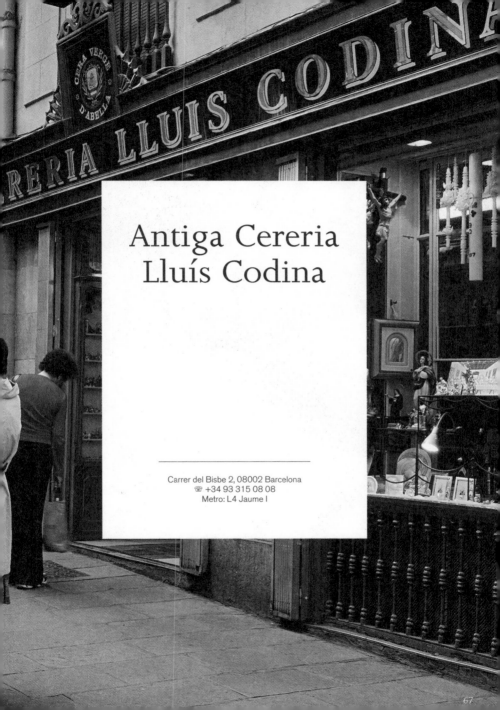

Antiga Cereria
Lluís Codina

Carrer del Bisbe 2, 08002 Barcelona
☎ +34 93 315 08 08
Metro: L4 Jaume I

VIRGEN DE GUADALUPE

Ntra. Sra. del Carmen

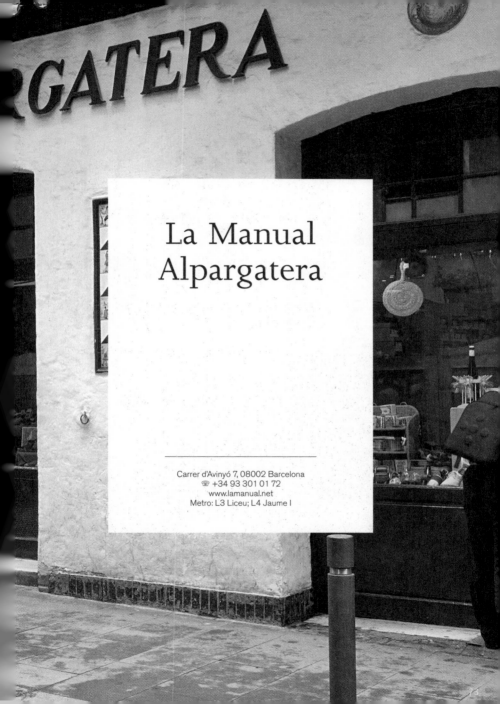

La Manual Alpargatera

Carrer d'Avinyó 7, 08002 Barcelona
☎ +34 93 301 01 72
www.lamanual.net
Metro: L3 Liceu; L4 Jaume I

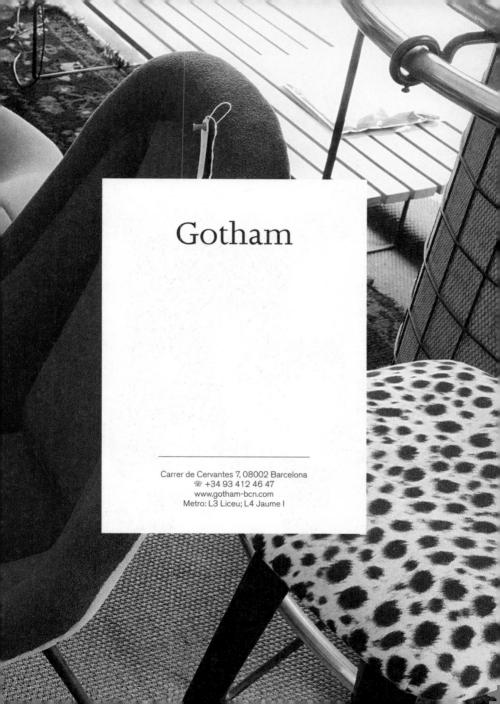

Gotham

Carrer de Cervantes 7, 08002 Barcelona
☎ +34 93 412 46 47
www.gotham-bcn.com
Metro: L3 Liceu; L4 Jaume I

Papabubble

Carrer Ample 28, 08002 Barcelona
☎ +34 93 268 86 25
www.papabubble.com
Metro: L3 Drassanes; L4 Jaume I

Cafés
El Magnífico

Carrer de l'Argenteria 64, 08003 Barcelona
☎ +34 93 310 33 61
www.cafeselmagnifico.com
Metro: L4 Jaume I

La Pelu

Carrer de l'Argenteria 70, 08003 Barcelona
☎ +34 93 310 48 07
www.lapelu.com
Metro: L4 Jaume I

BORREGUETS ｆ SANT ANTONI 250€

Brunells

Carrer de la Princesa 22, 08003 Barcelona
☎ +34 93 319 68 25
Metro: L4 Jaume I

30 Sable de tomàquet, orenga i parmesà:
Perquè tota una pizza seria massa. Requetebons.

la gal
de fib
es not
per di
i per f
molt
sanís

#17

Demasié

Carrer de la Princesa 28, 08003 Barcelona
☎ +34 93 310 42 95
www.demasie.es
Metro: L4 Jaume I

E & A Gispert

Carrer dels Sombrerers 23, 08003 Barcelona
☎ +34 93 319 75 35
www.casagispert.com
Metro: L4 Jaume I

VERD ÉS EL NOSTRE COLOR
FUMEJANT SÓN LES TORRADES
NO VINDRÀS ENDEBADES
TOT TÉ MOLT DE SABOR.

Targa

Pla de Palau 5–6, 08003 Barcelona
☎ +34 93 319 92 41
Metro: L4 Barceloneta

Lobby

Carrer de la Ribera 5, 08003 Barcelona
☎ +34 93 319 38 55
www.lobby-bcn.com
Metro: L4 Barceloneta; Jaume I

Xocoa

Carrer de Petritxol 11–13
08002 Barcelona
☏ +34 93 301 11 97

pp. 54/55

All about Chocolate
Interior: Minimalist; with a café

Open: Daily 9am–9pm | **X-Factor:** Ginger and lavender chocolate.
Xocoa sells excellent extravagantly flavoured chocolates in stylish packages – particularly attractive are the retro-designs.

Öffnungszeiten: Täglich 9–21 Uhr | **X-Faktor:** Schokolade mit Ingwer oder Lavendel.
Xocoa verkauft extravagant aromatisierte, exzellente Schokoladen in stylischen Verpackungen – besonders schön sind die Retro-Designs.

Horaires d'ouverture : Tous les jours 9h–21h | **Le « petit plus » :** Chocolat au gingembre ou à la lavende.
Xocoa vend d'excellents chocolats aux parfums extravagants. Leur emballage a du style et les designs rétro sont particulièrement beaux.

Caelum

Carrer de la Palla 8
08002 Barcelona
☏ +34 93 302 69 93

pp. 60/61

Divine Delicacies
Interior: Boutique with teashop

Open: Daily 10.30am–2pm and 5–9pm | **X-Factor:** Fine fare from monasteries.
The name says it all: Caelum is like heaven on earth, and sells delicacies produced in Spanish monasteries.

Öffnungszeiten: Täglich 10.30–14 und 17–21 Uhr | **X-Faktor:** Gutes aus Klöstern.
Der Name ist Programm: Caelum gleicht dem Himmel auf Erden und bietet Köstlichkeiten an, die in spanischen Klöstern hergestellt werden.

Horaires d'ouverture : Tous les jours 10h30–14h et 17h–21h | **Le « petit plus » :** Délices monastiques.
Le nom est tout un programme. Caelum, c'est le paradis sur terre et ses friandises sont préparées dans des monastères espagnols.

Antiga Cereria Lluis Codina

Carrer del Bisbe 2
08002 Barcelona
☏ +34 93 315 08 08

pp. 66/67

Catholic Devotional Objects
Interior: Original, dating from the 19th century

Open: Mo–Sa 9am–1.30pm and 4.30–7.45pm; Su 10am–1.30pm | **X-Factor:** Baptismal candles.
Spain from its religious side: this picturesque shop has statues of saints, rosary beads and candles.

Öffnungszeiten: Mo–Sa 9–13.30 und 16.30–19.45, So 10–13.30 Uhr | **X-Faktor:** Die Taufkerzen.
Hier zeigt sich Spanien von seiner religiösen Seite: Der malerische Laden führt Heiligenfiguren, Rosenkränze und Kerzen.

Horaires d'ouverture : Lun–Sam 9h–13h30 et 16h30–19h45, Dim 10h–13h30 | **Le « petit plus » :** Les cierges de baptême | L'Espagne se montre ici sous son côté religieux. Le pittoresque magasin propose des statuettes de saints, des chapelets et des cierges.

La Manual Alpargatera

Carrer d'Avinyó, 7
08002 Barcelona
☏ +34 93 301 01 72
www.lamanual.net

pp. 72/73

Handmade Spanish Espadrilles
Interior: Workshop atmosphere

Open: Daily 9.30am–1.30pm and 4.30–8pm | **X-Factor:** Excellent personal advice.
Classic, handmade espadrilles in all shades. Even Hollywood stars like Michael Douglas und Penélope Cruz wear them.

Öffnungszeiten: Täglich 9.30–13.30 und 16.30–20 Uhr | **X-Faktor:** Die perfekte und persönliche Beratung.
Klassische, handgefertigte Espadrilles in allen Farben. Diese Schuhe tragen selbst Hollywoodstars wie Michael Douglas und Penélope Cruz.

Horaires d'ouverture : Tous les jours 9h30–13h30 et 16h30–20h | **Le « petit plus » :** Service personnalisé et de qualité | Espadrilles classiques, fabriquées main. Même les stars d'Hollywood, comme Michael Douglas et Penélope Cruz, en raffolent.

Gotham

Carrer de Cervantes 7
08002 Barcelona
℡ +34 93 412 46 47
www.gotham-bcn.com

pp. 78/79

Vintage Furniture for Sale & Rent
Interior: Formerly a printer's

Open: Daily 10.30am–2pm and 5–8.30pm | **X-Factor:** The colourful restored 1950s Spanish furnitures.
Furniture from the 1950s, 1960s and 1970s. In demand by film directors – and Pedro Almodóvar is also a customer.

Öffnungszeiten: Täglich 10.30–14 und 17–20.30 Uhr | **X-Faktor:** Die bunten spanischen Möbel aus den 1950ern. Die Möbel stammen aus den 1950ern, 1960ern und 1970ern. Sie sind bei Regisseuren als Requisiten begehrt – auch Pedro Almodóvar ist Kunde.

Horaires d'ouverture : Tous les jours 10h30–14h et 17h–20h30 | **Le « petit plus » :** Les meubles espagnols colorés des années 1950. | Datant des années 1950 à 1970, ces meubles sont très recherchés par les réalisateurs pour leurs décors. Pedro Almodóvar fait lui aussi partie des clients de la maison.

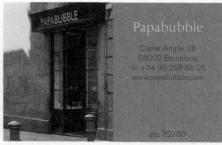

Papabubble

Carrer Ample 28
08002 Barcelona
℡ +34 93 268 86 25
www.papabubble.com

pp. 82/83

Homemade Sweets
Interior: Laboratory and shop all in one

Open: Tu–Fr 10am–2pm and 4–8.30pm; Sa 10am–8.30pm; Su 11am–7.30pm | **X-Factor:** The first sweet is always free! The sweets are made on site and have surprising tiny shapes and interesting flavours.

Öffnungszeiten: Di–Fr 10–14 und 16–20.30, Sa 10–20.30, So 11–19.30 Uhr | **X-Faktor:** Das erste Bonbon ist immer gratis!
Die Süßigkeiten werden direkt im Shop gefertigt und überraschen mit witzigen Formen sowie interessanten Aromen.

Horaires d'ouverture : Mar–Ven 10h–14h et 16h–20h30, Sam 10h–20h30, Dim 11h–19h30 | **Le « petit plus » :** Le premier bonbon est toujours gratis !
Directement préparées dans la boutique, les sucreries nous étonnent par leurs formes amusantes et leurs parfums inédits.

Cafes
El Magnifico

Carrer de l'Argenteria 64
08003 Barcelona
℡ +34 93 310 33 61
www.cafeselmagnifico.com

pp. 88/89

Perfectly Roasted Coffee, since 1919
Interior: Colonial

Open: Mo–Fr 9am–1.30pm and 4–8pm; Sa 10am–2pm | **X-Factor:** The tea shop "Sans & Sans" opposite.
Salvador Sans Velasco is the most famous coffee roaster in town and travels the world to select the best beans personally.

Öffnungszeiten: Mo–Fr 9–13.30 und 16–20, Sa 10–14 Uhr | **X-Faktor:** Der Teeladen „Sans & Sans" gegenüber.
Salvador Sans Velasco ist der bekannteste Kaffeeröster der Stadt und reist persönlich durch die Welt, um die besten Bohnen zu finden.

Horaires d'ouverture : Lun–Ven 9h–13h30 et 16h–20h, Sam 10h–14h | **Le « petit plus » :** Le magasin de thé « Sans & Sans » situé en face | Salvador Sans Velasco est le plus grand torréfacteur de la ville. Il parcourt le monde entier à la recherche des meilleurs grains de café.

La Pelu

Carrer de l'Argenteria 70
08003 Barcelona
℡ +34 93 310 48 07
www.lapelu.com

pp. 92/93

Extravagant Hairdresser's
Interior: With photo gallery

Open: Mo/Tu 10.30am–8pm; We 10.30am–9pm; Th/Fr 9.30am–9.30pm; Sa 11am–8pm | **X-Factor:** When there's a full moon, open 10pm–1.30am.
La Pelu is short for "La Peluquería" – and famous for asymmetrical cuts and striking colours.

Öffnungszeiten: Mo/Di 10.30–20, Mi 10.30–21, Do/Fr 9.30–21.30, Sa 11–20 Uhr | **X-Faktor:** Bei Vollmond ist von 22–1.30 Uhr geöffnet.
La Pelu ist die Abkürzung von „La Peluquería" – und für asymmetrische Schnitte sowie auffallende Farben bekannt.

Horaires d'ouverture : Lun/Mar 10h30–20h, Mer 10h30–21h, Jeu/Ven 9h30–21h30, Sam 11h–20h | **Le « petit plus » :** Ouvert de 22h à –1h30 les nuits de pleine lune.
La Pelu est l'abréviation de « La Peluquería » – et est célèbre pour ses coupes asymétriques et ses teintures tape-à-l'œil.

Brunells

Carrer de la Princesa 22
08003 Barcelona
☎ +34 93 319 68 25

pp. 96/97

Legendary Spanish Pastry
Interior: Original 1889

Open: Mo–Sa 8.30am–8pm | **X-Factor:** Fruit filled with ice cream.
The cakes and pastries, and even the famous meringue-like "Roques de Montserrat", have always been baked over a wood fire.

Öffnungszeiten: Mo–Sa 8.30–20 Uhr | **X-Faktor:** Die mit Eis gefüllten Früchte.
Seit jeher werden alle Kuchen und Kekse über Holzfeuer gebacken; auch die berühmten baiserähnlichen „Roques de Montserrat".

Horaires d'ouverture : Lun–Sam 8h30–20h | **Le « petit plus » :** Les fruits à la crème glacée.
Tous les gâteaux et biscuits sont cuits au feu de bois depuis toujours. Cela vaut aussi pour les fameux meringués, les « Roques de Montserrat ».

Demasié

Carrer de la Princesa 28
08003 Barcelona
☎ +34 93 310 42 95
www.demasie.es

pp. 102/103

Exquisite Sweet & Savoury Cookies
Interior: Minimalist

Open: Mo–Sa 10.30am–9pm; Su 12noon–8pm | **X-Factor:** The seductive aroma.
The traditional Catalan "galletas" are made by hand, often with modern refinements – for example, truffles, Roquefort, Sobrasada or curry.

Öffnungszeiten: Mo–Sa 10.30–21, So 12–20 Uhr | **X-Faktor:** Der verführerische Duft.
Die traditionellen katalanischen „galletas" werden von Hand hergestellt und oft modern verfeinert – etwa mit Trüffel, Roquefort, Sobrasada oder Curry.

Horaires d'ouverture : Lun–Sam 10h30–21h, Dim 12h–20h | **Le « petit plus » :** Le parfum enivrant | Les « galletas » catalanes sont cuites à la main d'après une recette traditionnelle, à partir de laquelle sont déclinées des variantes plus modernes, comme celles à la truffe, au roquefort, à la sobrasada ou au curry.

E & A Gispert

Carrer dels Sombrerers 23
08003 Barcelona
☎ +34 93 319 75 35
www.casagispert.com

pp. 106/107

Dried Fruits & Roasted Nuts
Interior: Original, dating from 1851

Open: Tu–Fr 9.30am–2pm and 4–7.30pm; Sa 10am–2pm and 5–8pm | **X-Factor:** The selection of wines.
More than 150 years ago, Gispert were selling exotic products from overseas – today they specialise in nuts and fruits roasted and dried in an antique oven.

Öffnungszeiten: Di–Fr 9.30–14 und 16–19.30, Sa 10–14 und 17–20 Uhr | **X-Faktor:** Die Weinauswahl.
Vor 150 Jahren bot Gispert Exotisches aus Übersee an – heute Nüsse und Obstsorten, die vor Ort in einem antiken Ofen geröstet und gedörrt werden.

Horaires d'ouverture : Mar–Ven 9h30–14h et 16h–19h30, Sam 10h–14h et 17h–20h | **Le « petit plus » :** Le choix des vins | Il y a 150 ans Gispert proposait des produits exotiques, aujourd'hui il vend des noix et des fruits qui sont grillés et séchés dans un très vieux four.

Targa

Pla de Palau 5–6
08003 Barcelona
☎ +34 93 319 92 41

pp. 112/113

Mediterranean Kitchenware
Interior: Orderly

Open: Mo–Fr 9am–1.30pm and 4–8pm; Sa 9am–12noon | **X-Factor:** Pots whose handles do not heat up when used on a gas hobs.
From the paella pan to the espresso pot – here you can get the basics for Spanish and Mediterranean cuisine.

Öffnungszeiten: Mo–Fr 9–13.30 und 16–20 Uhr, Sa 9–12 Uhr | **X-Faktor:** Die Töpfe für den Gasherd, deren Griffe nicht heiß werden.
Von der Paellapfanne bis zur Espressokanne: Hier gibt es die „basics" für jede spanische und mediterrane Küche.

Horaires d'ouverture : Lun–Ven 9h–13h30 et 16h–20h, Sam 9h–12h | **Le « petit plus » :** Les casseroles pour la gazinière dont les poignées ne prennent pas la chaleur. Poêle à paella, cafetière expresso, vous trouverez ici tous les ustensiles pour la cuisine espagnole et méditerranéenne.

Lobby

Carrer de la Ribera 5
08003 Barcelona
℡ +34 93 319 38 55
www.lobby-bcn.com

pp. 116/117

Chic Concept Store
Interior: Modern design inside old walls

Open: Mo–Sa 11am–9pm | **X-Factor:** The själ beauty
products.
In addition to trendy fashions by international and Spanish
designers such as Jaume Roca or Txell Miras, the Concept
Store also sells cosmetics and books.

Öffnungszeiten: Mo–Sa 11–21 Uhr | **X-Faktor:** Die
Beautyprodukte von själ.
Neben Trend-Mode von internationalen und spanischen
Designern wie Jaume Roca oder Txell Miras bietet der
Concept Store auch Kosmetik und Bücher.

Horaires d'ouverture : Lun–Sam 11h–21h | **Le « petit
plus » :** Les produits de beauté de själ.
Ce concept store propose à côté de la mode tendance de
créateurs internationaux et espagnols, comme Jaume Roca
ou Txell Miras, des produits de cosmétique et des livres.

123

L'Eixample
Gràcia
Sant Gervasi

128 Travel books/Reiseliteratur/Livres de voyage
Llibreria Altaïr

132 Spanish leather goods/Spanische Lederwaren/Maroquinerie espagnole
Loewe

136 Flowers around the clock/24-Stunden-Blumen/Fleurs 24h/24
Floristería Navarro

140 Spanish ham/Spanischer Schinken/Jambon d'Espagne
Charcuterías Joaquín Gracia

146 Spanish fashion/Spanische Mode/Mode espagnole
Josep Font

150 Legendary design shop/Legendärer Designshop/Designshop légendaire
Vinçon

156 Photography books & gallery/Fotografie-Bücher & Galerie/
Livres de photographie & galerie
Kowasa

160 Furniture & more/Möbel & more/Mobilier & plus
Coriumcasa

166 Spanish shoes/Spanische Schuhe/Chaussures espagnoles
Camper

170 Fashion/Designermode/Mode
Jean Pierre Symbol

174 Fashion/Mode/Mode
Jean Pierre Bua

180 Sexy espadrilles/Sexy Espadrilles/Espadrilles sexy
Cristina Castañer

184 Chocolate/Schokolade/Chocolats
Oriol Balaguer

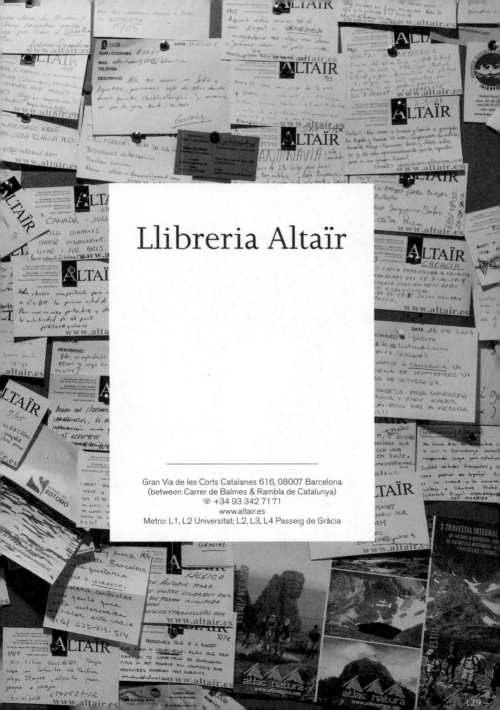

Llibreria Altaïr

Gran Via de les Corts Catalanes 616, 08007 Barcelona
(between Carrer de Balmes & Rambla de Catalunya)
☎ +34 93 342 71 71
www.altair.es
Metro: L1, L2 Universitat; L2, L3, L4 Passeig de Gràcia

Loewe

Passeig de Gràcia 35, 08007 Barcelona
☎ +34 93 216 04 00
www.loewe.es
Metro: L2, L3, L4 Passeig de Gràcia

Floristería Navarro

Carrer de València 320, 08009 Barcelona
☎ +34 93 207 36 61
www.floristeriasnavarro.com
Metro: L4 Girona; L4, L5 Verdaguer

Jamon bodega
de Teruel
22'50 €/k

Jar

16

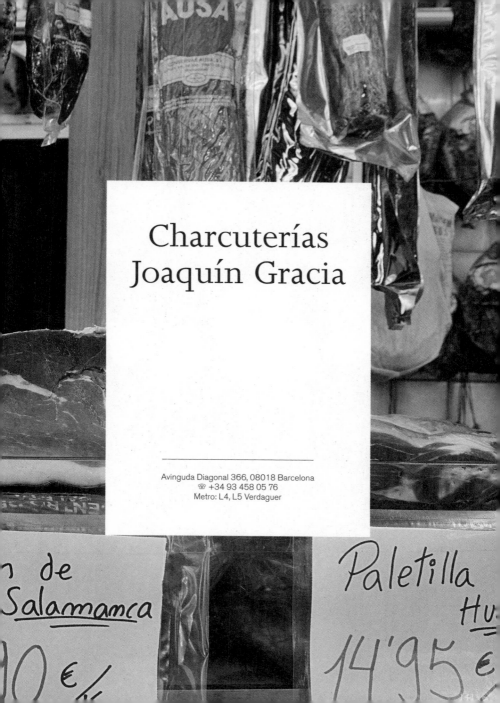

Charcuterías Joaquín Gracia

Avinguda Diagonal 366, 08018 Barcelona
☏ +34 93 458 05 76
Metro: L4, L5 Verdaguer

JOSEP FONT

Josep Font

Carrer de Provença 304, 08008 Barcelona
☎ +34 93 487 21 10
www.josepfont.com
Metro: L3, L5 Diagonal

Vinçon

Passeig de Gràcia 96, 08008 Barcelona
☎ +34 93 215 60 50
www.vincon.com
Metro: L3, L5 Diagonal

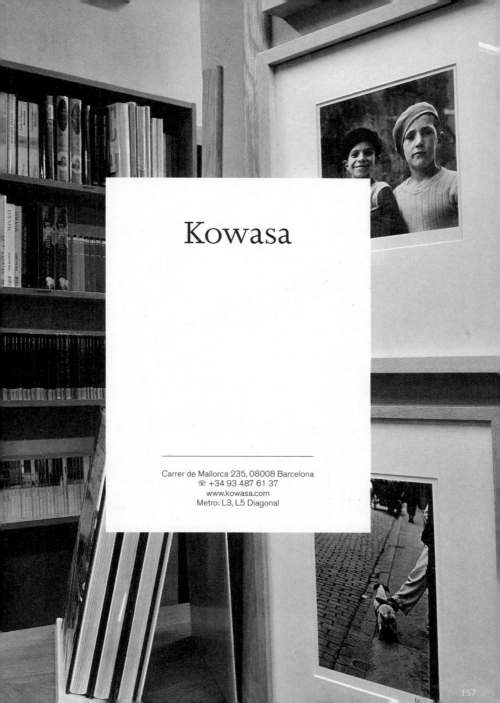

Kowasa

Carrer de Mallorca 235, 08008 Barcelona
☎ +34 93 487 61 37
www.kowasa.com
Metro: L3, L5 Diagonal

Coriumcasa

Carrer de Provença 268, 08008 Barcelona
☎ +34 93 272 12 24
www.coriumcasa.com
Metro: L3, L5 Diagonal

Camper

Carrer de Muntaner 248, 08021 Barcelona
☎ +34 93 201 31 88
www.camper.es
Metro: L5 Hospital Clínic; L3, L5 Diagonal

Jean Pierre Symbol

Avinguda Diagonal 467, 08036 Barcelona
☎ +34 93 444 49 62
www.jeanpierresymbol.com
Metro: L5 Hospital Clínic

Jean Pierre Bua

Avinguda Diagonal 469, 08036 Barcelona
☎ +34 93 439 71 00
www.jeanpierrebua.com
Metro: L5 Hospital Clíníc

Cristina
Castañer

Carrer del Mestre Nicolau 23, 08021 Barcelona
☏ +34 93 414 24 28
www.castaner.com
Metro: L6 Muntaner

Oriol Balaguer

Plaça de Sant Gregori Taumaturg 2, 08021 Barcelona
☏ +34 93 201 18 46
www.oriolbalaguer.com
Metro: L6 La Bonanova/Muntaner

Llibreria Altaïr

Gran Via de les Corts
Catalanes 616
(between Carrer de Balmes &
Rambla de Catalunya)
08007 Barcelona
☎ +34 93 342 71 71
www.altair.es

pp. 128/129

Travel Books & Guides
Interior: Exotic flair

Open: Mo–Sa 10am–2pm and 4.30–8.30pm | **X-Factor:**
Biographies of famous travellers.
An amazing range of travel literature and maps – discover
the whole world on a small number of square metres.

Öffnungszeiten: Mo–Sa 10–14 und 16.30–20.30 Uhr |
X-Faktor: Die Biografien großer Reisender.
Ein sagenhaftes Sortiment an Reiseliteratur und Landkarten
– auf wenigen Quadratmetern entdeckt man die ganze Welt.

Horaires d'ouverture : Lun–Sam 10h–14 et 16h30–
20h30 | **Le « petit plus » :** Les biographies des grands
explorateurs.
Un incroyable choix de livres de voyage et de cartes ! Sur
quelques mètres carrés on découvre ici le monde entier.

Loewe

Passeig de Gràcia 35
08007 Barcelona
☎ +34 93 216 04 00
www.loewe.es

pp. 132/133

Luxurious Leather Accessories & Fashion
Interior: A Modernisme building by Domènech (1905)

Open: Mo–Sa 10am–8.30pm | **X-Factor:** Only napa is used
for the leather goods.
A symbol of luxury in Spain since 1846 – and an exciting
mixture of bourgeois style and sexy glamour.

Öffnungszeiten: Mo–Sa 10–20.30 Uhr | **X-Faktor:** Für
die Lederwaren wird nur Nappaleder verwendet.
Seit 1846 ein Symbol für Luxus in Spanien – und eine
spannende Mischung aus bourgeoisem Glanz und sexy
Glamour.

Horaires d'ouverture : Lun–Sam 10h–20h30 | **Le « petit
plus » :** Tous les articles en cuir sont en cuir nappa.
Symbole du luxe en Espagne depuis 1846, offre un excitant
mélange de splendeur bourgeoise et de glamour sexy.

Floristería Navarro

Carrer de València 320
08009 Barcelona
☎ +34 93 207 36 61
www.floristeriasnavarro.com

pp. 136/137

Flowers on 800 Square Metres – 24 Hours a Day
Interior: The country-home style counter

Open: 24 hours a day | **X-Factor:** Fruit baskets arranged
like bouquets of flowers.
In Spain's largest "floristería", 100 people supervise a veritable
sea of flowers. The roses are legendary!

Öffnungszeiten: Täglich 24 Stunden | **X-Faktor:** Die wie
Sträuße arrangierten Obstkörbe.
In der größten „floristería" Spaniens kümmern sich 100
Mitarbeiter um ein Blumenmeer. Die Rosen sind legendär!

Horaires d'ouverture : Tous les jours 24h/24 | **Le « petit
plus » :** Les corbeilles de fruits arrangées comme des
bouquets | Une centaine d'employés s'occupent d'une mer
de fleurs dans cette « floristería », la plus grande d'Espagne.
Les roses y sont légendaires !

Charcuterías Joaquín Gracia

Avinguda Diagonal 366
08018 Barcelona
☎ +34 93 458 05 76

pp. 140/141

Delicious Spanish Ham
Interior: Like a film set – almost surreal

Open: Daily 8.30am–2pm and 5–9pm | **X-Factor:** The ham
"pata negra".
A fantastic selection of hams from all over Spain – all treated
by hand and sliced paper-thin.

Öffnungszeiten: Täglich 8.30–14 und 17–21 Uhr |
X-Faktor: Der Schinken „pata negra".
Eine fantastische Auswahl an Hinterschinken aus ganz
Spanien – alle von Hand hergestellt und hauchdünn ge-
schnitten.

Horaires d'ouverture : Tous les jours 8h30–14h et
17h–21h | **Le « petit plus » :** Le jambon « pata negra »
Un choix fantastique de jambons de toutes les régions
d'Espagne. Tous sont faits maison et coupés en tranches
ultra fines.

Josep Font

Carrer de Provença 304
08008 Barcelona
☎ +34 93 487 21 10
www.josepfont.com

pp. 146/147

Contemporary Spanish Designer Fashion
Interior: Traditional mosaic floor

Open: Mo–Sa 10am–8.30pm | **X-Factor:** One of Spain's
most interesting fashion designers.
Josep Font's creations have a touch of the romantic – and
really stand out in this generously spaced shop.

Öffnungszeiten: Mo–Sa 10–20.30 Uhr | **X-Faktor:** Einer
der interessantesten spanischen Mode-Designer.
Die Kreationen von Josep Font sind romantisch angehaucht
– und kommen im großzügigen Shop gut zur Geltung.

Horaires d'ouverture : Lun–Sam 10h–20h30 | **Le « petit
plus » :** L'un des designers espagnols les plus intéressants.
Un brin romantiques, les créations de Josep Font ont trouvé
une place idéale dans cette vaste boutique.

Vinçon

Passeig de Gràcia 96
08008 Barcelona
☎ +34 93 215 60 50
www.vincon.com

pp. 150/151

Contemporary Designer Furniture & Accessories
Interior: A splendid building with a bel étage (1899; Antonio
Rovira y Rabassa)

Open: Mo–Sa 10am–8.30pm | **X-Factor:** The designer
bags are collector's items.
More than 10,000 designer objects on three floors – every-
thing you could possibly need for your home.

Öffnungszeiten: Mo–Sa 10–20.30 Uhr | **X-Faktor:** Die
von Künstlern entworfenen Tüten sind Sammlerstücke.
Mehr als 10.000 Designobjekte auf drei Etagen – alles, was
man für sein Heim benötigt.

Horaires d'ouverture : Lun–Sam 10h–20h30 | **Le « petit
plus » :** Les sacs dessinés par des artistes sont devenus des
objets de collection.
Plus de 10 000 objets design répartis sur trois étages – tous
les articles de maison possibles et imaginables.

Kowasa

Carrer de Mallorca 235
08008 Barcelona
☎ +34 93 487 61 37
www.kowasa.com

pp. 156/157

Books on Photography
Interior: Functional

Open: Daily 11am–2pm and 5–8.30pm | **X-Factor:** Original
photographs are also available.
Kowasa's stocks include more than 12,000 photography
books – a European record. The photography gallery is also
worth a visit.

Öffnungszeiten: Täglich 11–14 und 17–20.30 Uhr |
X-Faktor: Auch gute Originalfotografien erhältlich.
Kowasas Sortiment umfasst mehr als 12.000 Titel an Foto-
grafiebüchern – das ist Europarekord. Auch die Fotogalerie
lohnt einen Besuch.

Horaires d'ouverture : Tous les jours 11h–14h et 17h–
20h30 | **Le « petit plus » :** De bons clichés originaux sont
également disponibles. | Kowasa propose plus de 12 000 liv-
res de photographie, ce qui constitue un record en Europe.
La galerie de photos vaut elle aussi le détour.

Coriumcasa

Carrer de Provença 268
08008 Barcelona
☎ +34 93 272 12 24
www.coriumcasa.com

pp. 160/161

Selected Designer Furniture
Interior: Beautifully renovated historical building

Open: Mo–Sa 10am–2pm and 4.30–8.30pm | **X-Factor:** Its
sistershop ("Corium", Passeig de Gràcia 106).
Their fine selection of well-designed furniture is comple-
mented by matching blankets, cushions and ceramics.

Öffnungszeiten: Mo–Sa 10–14 und 16.30–20.30 Uhr |
X-Faktor: Mit Schwesterladen („Corium", Passeig de Gràcia
106).
Die feine Auswahl an formschönen Möbeln wird durch
passende Decken, Kissen und Keramik ergänzt.

Horaires d'ouverture : Lun–Sam 10h–14h et 16h30–
20h30 | **Le « petit plus » :** Avec la boutique jumelle
(« Corium », Passeig de Gràcia 106).
Couvertures, coussins et céramiques viennent compléter avec
bonheur cette sélection de meubles aux formes agréables.

Camper

Carrer de Muntaner 248
08021 Barcelona
☏ +34 93 201 31 88
www.camper.es

pp. 166/167

Easygoing Spanish Shoes
Interior: Uncomplicated, sporty

Open: Mo–Sa 10am–2pm and 4–8pm | **X-Factor:** The imaginative children's shoe collection.
Lorenzo Fluxà designed the first Camper shoe in 1975 – the brand is a source of national pride today. This was the first shop worldwide.

Öffnungszeiten: Mo–Sa 10–14 und 16–20 Uhr |
X-Faktor: Die fantasievolle Kinderschuh-Kollektion.
Lorenzo Fluxà entwarf den ersten Camper-Schuh 1975 – heute ist die Marke ein Nationalstolz. Dieser Laden war der erste weltweit.

Horaires d'ouverture : Lun–Sam 10h–14h et 16h–20h |
Le « petit plus » : La collection pour enfants pleine d'originalité | Lorenzo Fluxà a créé la première chaussure Camper en 1975 – depuis, la marque fait la fierté du pays. Ce magasin fut le premier dans le monde entier.

Jean Pierre Symbol

Avinguda Diagonal 467
08036 Barcelona
☏ +34 93 444 49 62
www.jeanpierresymbol.com

pp. 170/171

Casual Designer Fashion
Interior: Sophisticated

Open: Mo–Sa 10am–2pm and 4.30–8.30pm | **X-Factor:** The latest Bua Boutique in Barcelona.
On three spacious floors you will find casual fashions by avant-garde designers with matching shoes and accessories.

Öffnungszeiten: Mo–Sa 10–14 und 16.30–20.30 Uhr |
X-Faktor: Die neueste Bua-Boutique in Barcelona.
Auf drei weitläufigen Etagen findet man die Casual-Mode avantgardistischer Designer samt passender Schuhe und Accessoires.

Horaires d'ouverture : Lun–Sam 10h–14h et 16h30–20h30 | **Le « petit plus » :** La toute nouvelle boutique Bua à Barcelone | Sur trois étages spacieux, une mode casual de créateurs d'avant-garde ainsi que les chaussures et les accessoires qui vont avec.

Jean Pierre Bua

Avinguda Diagonal 469
08036 Barcelona
☏ +34 93 439 71 00
www.jeanpierrebua.com

pp. 174/175

Avant-garde Designer Fashion
Design: Margarita Viarnés & Rosendo Cortés

Open: Mo–Sa 10am–2pm and 4.30–8.30pm | **X-Factor:** Established for more than 20 years.
French owner Jean Pierre Bua stocks haute couture that fills the Spanish with enthusiasm – for example, by Jean Paul Gaultier, Stella McCartney and Martin Margiela.

Öffnungszeiten: Mo–Sa 10–14 und 16.30–20.30 Uhr |
X-Faktor: Etabliert seit mehr als 20 Jahren.
Der Franzose Jean Pierre Bua begeistert die Spanier für Haute Couture – z. B. von Jean Paul Gaultier, Stella McCartney und Martin Margiela.

Horaires d'ouverture : Lun–Sam 10h–14h et 16h30–20h30 | **Le « petit plus » :** Réputé depuis plus de vingt ans. Grâce au Français Jean Pierre Bua, les Espagnols raffolent de la haute-couture et des grands couturiers comme Jean Paul Gaultier, Stella McCartney et Martin Margiela.

Cristina Castañer

Carrer del Mestre Nicolau 23
08021 Barcelona
☏ +34 93 414 24 28
www.castaner.com

pp. 180/181

Glamorous Espadrilles
Interior: Ample space for the complete collection

Open: Mo–Sa 10.30am–8.15pm | **X-Factor:** Evening shoes with huge bows.
Castañer hit the catwalks and the cover pages in the 1960s with a commission by YSL for high-heel espadrilles.

Öffnungszeiten: Mo–Sa 10.30–20.15 Uhr | **X-Faktor:** Die Abendschuhe mit großen Schleifen.
Mit YSL's Auftrag zu High-Heel-Espadrilles brachte es Castañer in den 1960ern auf den Catwalk und internationale Coverseiten.

Horaires d'ouverture : Lun–Sam 10h30–20h15 |
Le « petit plus » : Les chaussures de soirée avec leurs grosses boucles | Grâce aux espadrilles à hauts talons commandées jadis par YSL, Castañer a trouvé le chemin des défilés de mode et des couvertures des magazines internationaux.

Oriol Balaguer

Plaça de Sant Gregori
Taumaturg 2
08021 Barcelona
☎ +34 93 201 18 46
www.oriolbalaguer.com

pp. 184/185

Finest Pralinés & Pastry
Design: GCA Arquitectes, Barcelona

Open: Mo–Sa 10am–2.30pm and 5–9pm; Su 10am–
12.30pm | **X-Factor:** The nine varieties of the "BCN
Collection". | His father was a pâtissier and passed on his
passion to his son: Oriol Balaguer's prize-winning chocolates
are extremely stylishly packed.

Öffnungszeiten: Mo–Sa 10–14.30 und 17–21, So 10–
12.30 Uhr | **X-Faktor:** Die „BCN Collection" mit neun Sorten.
Sein Vater war Pâtissier und vererbte ihm seine Passion:
Oriol Balaguers Schokoladen sind preisgekrönt und äußerst
stilvoll verpackt.

Horaires d'ouverture : Lun–Sam 10h–14h30 et 17h–21h,
Dim 10h–12h30 | **Le « petit plus » :** La « BCN Collection »
aux neuf parfums.
Oriol Balaguer tient sa passion de son père pâtissier : ses
chocolats sont primés et emballés avec beaucoup d'élégance.

© 2007 TASCHEN GmbH
Hohenzollernring 53, D-50672 Köln
www.taschen.com

Compilation, Editing & Layout
Angelika Taschen, Berlin

General Project Manager
Stephanie Bischoff, Cologne

Photos
Pep Escoda, Tarragona

Cover Illustration
Olaf Hajek, www.olafhajek.com

Maps
dieSachbearbeiter.*innen*, Berlin

Graphic Design
Eggers + Diaper, Berlin

Captions
Christiane Reiter, Hamburg

French Translation
Thérèse Chatelain-Südkamp, Cologne

English Translation
Pauline Cumbers, Frankfurt am Main

Lithograph Manager
Thomas Grell, Cologne

Printed in Italy
ISBN 978-3-8365-0055-5

To stay informed about upcoming TASCHEN titles, please request our magazine at www.taschen.com/magazine or write to TASCHEN, Hohenzollernring 53, D-50672 Cologne, Germany, contact@taschen.com, Fax: +49 221 25 49 19. We will be happy to send you a free copy of our magazine which is filled with information about all our books.